retired boots

A collection of poems from a Route 91 survivor

WRITTEN BY:
DR. MORGAN JEAN CRAIG BELKNAP
ART BY: TIKVA

retired boots

"He will cover you with His feathers

and under His wings you will find refuge

His faithfulness will be your shield and rampart

you will not fear the terror of night

nor the arrow that flies by day

nor the pestilence that stalks in the darkness

nor the plague that destroys at midday

a thousand may fall at your side

ten thousand at your right hand

but it will not come near you"

psalm 91:4-7
new international version
The Holy Bible

dedication

to my God, for protecting me that night,

to my husband for loving the most broken parts of me,

to my children for reminding me of the

innocence of the world,

to my family and friends for standing by me

with endless support,

to my therapist for listening to everything and giving me

homework to write letters on my healing journey,

to my church family for the friendship, love, and prayers,

to those that texted me that life-shaking night,

to those that checked in on me on the following days,

to those that check in with me every October 1st,

to those that check in with me after every mass shooting.

        thank you, with everything I am.

I am in awe that this book has come together like it has.

I had a collection of poems, writings, and letters, that I had written, and tucked away. Much like I tucked myself away. I felt like I didn't want to share in fear of hurting others with my pain. February 14, 2024, as yet another mass shooting took place, I cried in my husband's arms. And like a mustard seed of faith, I became even more vulnerable and asked my husband if he wanted to see my poems, writings, and letters. He opened his heart and mind to my painful art. After reading and investing his emotional energy, his reactions, along with the Holy Spirit, placed it on my heart. I needed to publish this work. I needed to share these pains with the world. I then was filled with all of the ideas and components to create this beautifully vulnerable and raw work of art.

My hope is that this book helps others empathize and understand the pain that continues to exist within the heart and mind of survivors of mass shootings. My other hope is that other survivors feel less alone with their pain.

-Morgan Jean

warning

Please be advised that the content of this book may be disturbing to some. Themes include blood, death, violence, gun violence, mass shooting, trauma, and other emotions. This book also includes explicit language due to the nature of the real and raw nature of these written pieces.
If this is upsetting to you, please be advised to seek out support.

To anyone who has also experienced a mass shooting, whether directly or secondhand impact, this may bring up unresolved issues. Seek therapeutic support as needed, and be aware of the resources in your area for mental health.

9.29.2017

contents

denial..11

anger..27

bargaining..37

depression..49

acceptance..61

author's note

The weird thing about trauma, about grief, about pain, is that when we think of it as a concept, we envision these stages that categorize the thoughts and feelings that occur as our mind starts to grasp reality.

The issue with that, is that as we wake up each day, and go from moment to moment, we are struck with uncertainty of the emotional state we will be in from one moment to the next. A morning filled with anger and rage can move forward to an afternoon filled with sadness and depression.

Much like life, these poems are intentionally scattered, with some categorization. Each poem in each section was written at a different time, none of them parallel to each other. Healing is not linear, and neither is the progression of healing in this collection of poems.

DENIAL

it hurts still

but not like you think it might

it hurts to sit in the light

knowing your heart and mind

are in the shadows

it hurts to say i'm okay

when i'm really not

it hurts to see others with joy

in moments when I'm without

i'm brought back to moments of panic

it hurts to pretend that it doesn't hurt

it hurts still

everyone was fighting for their life

why should anyone try to protect mine?

i'll cover my own back

no one is coming to my rescue

i am on my own

if i make it out alive

i'll be so fucked up

                                        take deep breaths honey

                                              you are not alone

alone

october 1st, 2017

the roar of my favorite music filled my body and

fulfilled my soul

the crowd of people around me felt comforting

the lights flashing awakened the fire within me

the pounding bass and drums beating within my chest

it was just another concert

until it wasn't

i still remember that moment the switch was flipped

the moment just another concert

turned into a war zone

the moment when the gunfire began

the moment when i knew that it was not fireworks

even though everyone around me said it was

...

...

the moment when the music stopped

the moment i was told to get down

protect yourself

the moment when i crawled

through cigarette butts and spilled bud light cans

save yourself

keep crawling

clothes covered in cigarette ashes

i don't smoke

clothes covered in bud light

i'm more of a jack girl

i'm going to die

smelling of cigarettes and bud light

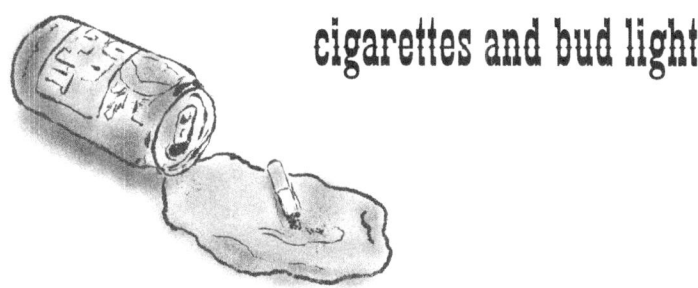

cigarettes and bud light

music.

fireworks.

those aren't fireworks.

gunshots.

screams.

dial tone.

begging God to save me.

screams.

gunshots.

silence.

silence.

silence.

silence

tension in my chest

feeling

stressed

stressed

stressed

jittery hands

shaking foot

shallow breaths

breathe in but its not deep enough

try again, one more time

this is the one thing i can control

but not enough

keep trying

your breathing is controllable

focus

on

that

anxiety

my mother gave me life

i'm staring at death

i need to call

i need to say goodbye

i keep calling

call dropped

people dropping

around me

i need to say goodbye

if i am going to drop too

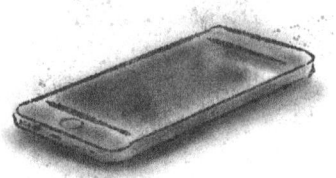

call dropped

not me

not now

not ever

God please

save me from this hell

save me from this pouring rain

i am done

i can't handle it

begging

i crawled

i ran

i hid

i was quiet

i still wasn't safe

i ran

i hid

i was quiet

barricade the door

we are never safe

drunk on life

drunk on bud light

drunk on the music

shots ring constant

sober on fear

sober on silence

sober on death

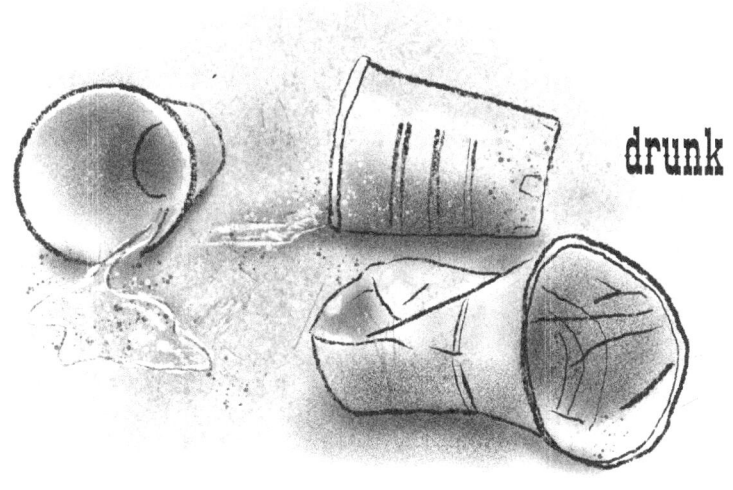

scrolling through instagram

vacation

daily routine

normal

scrolling through instagram

another shooting

how many injured?

how many killed?

normal.

normal

we were living

we were singing along

we were drinking

we were loving

we were lifting up our flag

he was lurking

he was preying

he was wanting

to call war on our peace

lurking

i am sorry

you will continue to hurt

i am sorry

we weren't supposed to see the worst

i am sorry

you were supposed to be safe

i am sorry

we should not have this in common

i am sorry

you don't know me

i don't know you

but we are now family

in a broken and shattered way

ANGER

showers of blood

                                        i saw too much

sprays of beer

                                        i smelled too much

wailing screams

                                        i heard too much

desperate pleas for life

                                        i felt too much

                why are we here again?

                we haven't had enough.

blood and beer

you're trying to let out your screams

but someone is sitting on your chest

fear

fear has you in her grips

keep trying

keep screaming

everyone can hear you

no one can save you

fear

they forgot again

didn't they?

back to the routine

back to the norm

advocating to get over it

i guess it's not trendy anymore

i haven't forgotten

you're not alone

we are still struggling

while they are forgetting

but i guess

life

goes

on.

life goes on

let her anger be known

as it crashes on down

calmness escapes

as it crashes down

hell hath no fury like her

when she is pissed and ignored

listen

just fucking listen

she cries

i'm not okay

i am broken, my waves have crashed

i am done

i am done

but i'm not

because tomorrow

you'll be back to appreciate my calmness

but you need to remember

my waves are intense yet forgiving

until they are not.

grief like an ocean

you don't care

stop pretending you do

you don't care

you weren't there

you didn't see what i saw

stop pretending like you care

your heart breaks yet you forget so quickly

sit with me

please sit with me

please fucking sit with me

you can't fix this

i can't fix this

but i'm so lonely in my own mind.

lonely

i don't want to be around anyone

but i don't want to be alone

i don't want to talk about it

but all i want to do is talk about it

i don't want anyone to bring it up

but i am waiting for someone to bring it up

i don't want your advice

but i don't know what to do

i don't want to go to work

but i can't stay in my room all day

i don't want to sleep all day

but my nightmares exhaust me

paradox

the deepest parts of me feel broken

and i have to go on

it is hard to go outside

it is hard to stay inside my head

there's too much noise

there's too many people

i don't feel safe

i am shattered

as my loved ones

tiptoe

over

the

broken

pieces

i can't let my broken edges cut them

i am a risk to love

because the deepest parts of me have been broken

broken edges

BARGAINING

turn the music down

turn the fucking music down

are those fireworks?

those aren't fireworks

the music stopped

turn the music back on

turn back time to when the music

 was the only sound

get down on the ground

turn the music down

our war starts now

turn the music down

why me

 why us

why this night

why this concert

why

why

why

why

everyone has their theory

everyone thinks they know what happened

i was there, and i don't know what happened

why do we care

why do we crave information

that won't change

won't change a thing

won't stop my heart from hurting

won't bring people back to life

 it won't change a thing for me

why do we care

okay

i'm done

i'm screaming

i

am

done

you can wake me up now

please wake me up

i am stuck

in this nightmare

a night terror

paralyzed by fear

please

oh please

wake me up

wake me up

God,

i will use this

please use me

please heal me

please heal the brokenness

please help me stop hurting

i am crying out for you

this hurts too much

i will do anything

anything

anything

but please don't make me go through this

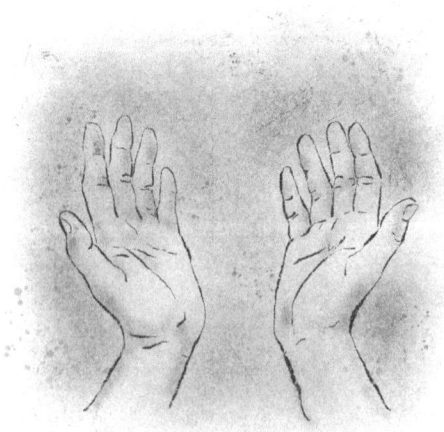

God, please

maybe this is my path

maybe this was meant to happen

why was this meant to happen

why was this meant to happen

maybe but why

it's not up to us to

u

n

d

e

r

s

t

a

n

d

understand

everyone has a story

you ask about mine

what a horrific story

enough to silence a room

enough to stun a crowd

enough to drum up a buzz

but that was my life

that was my sunday night

and it is a horrific story

i am stuck

stuck

stuck

stuck

i am broken

broken

broken

broken

i am hurt

hurt

hurt

hurt

and i cant change a damn thing.

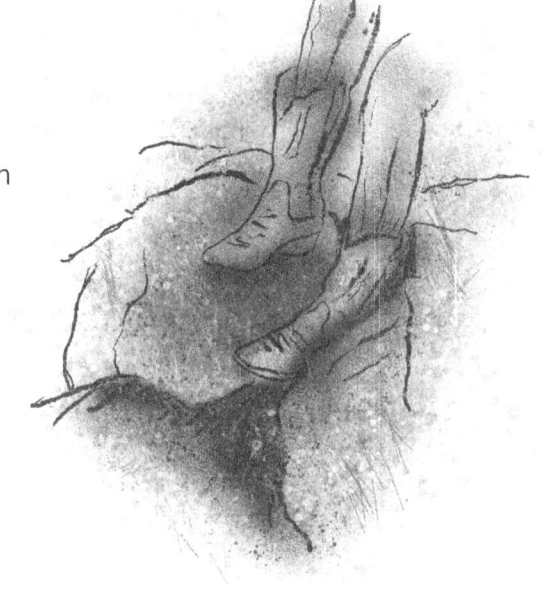

stuck

don't feel bad for me

don't pity me

please accept my no

and keep inviting me

i know i am hard to love right now

i know i am not fun

i know my spark has been extinguished

i know i am depressing to be around

please still love me

please don't forget about me

DEPRESSION

God

i feel so broken

i look up at the skylight

i can't distract my mind

i am stuck

i am broken

i don't want anyone or anything

i just want to cry

and lay here

stuck in this body

stuck in this mind

it feels so foreign to me

i don't recognize her

i dont want to recognize her

where has the old me gone?

i need her back

i am lost without her

where did she go

breaking news

it rained last night

and it poured

our umbrellas didn't stand a chance

it rained last night

the bullet kind of rain

the gun kind of clouds

it rained last night

i'm shaking

but I'm not cold

somebody please bring me a jacket

it rained last night

and i'm still shaking

flag at half-mast

thoughts and prayers

it rained last night

i can still hear the downfall

hit the ground

those are people

hitting the ground

...

...

it rained last night

flag half-mast

thoughts and prayers

i can still feel it in my chest

i'm shaking

flag half-mast

thoughts and prayers

when i go into a crowd

most people haven't experienced this rain

 it rained last night

and they just see me shaking on a sunny day

pitying that i am still cold

pitying that i felt the rain last night

flag half-mast

thoughts and prayers

i may not know how to stop the rain but...

breaking news **it rained last night**

sandbags tied to your feet,

and you're emptying the bags

grain

by

grain

they must feel so heavy

but know

they are lighter than they were

yesterday

last week

last month

last year

see the beauty in the lightness of your steps

let yourself run a marathon

let yourself skip and jump

and embrace being light

let your lightness bring lightness in

grain

by

grain

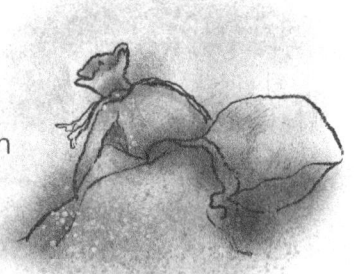

sandbags

there was a shooting

i am shocked yet not

injuries reported

the bullets fell

my tears fall

death confirmed

my eyes fill

another death

vision is blurred

the death toll rises

my eyes cry

the death toll rises

my body sobs

the death toll rises

my soul sobs

58 lives lost

my heart breaks

2 more lives lost

my soul continues to ache

sobbing

i heard you were in Vegas?

                                        the tears fall

oh you're already back to work?

                                        the tears fall

did you think there was a second shooter?

                                        the tears fall

what do you think about gun control?

                                        the tears fall

why are you on crutches?

                                        the tears fall

why do you flinch so much?

                                        the tears fall

why are you crying?

                                        the tears fall

tears

as time goes on

the lonelier we get

yet the more connected we get

                                      it's been 6 years

                              you aren't over it yet?

no

of course not

because it is still happening

some have pushed it deep down

while others are running for their life

it's been 6 years and i am still running for my life

lonelier we get

to my family and friends,

thank you for the love

thank you for the support

know you don't have to fix me

know you don't have to change me

know you don't have to have the right words

know you don't need to say anything

know you can

just

hold

space

support

ACCEPTANCE

hi there las vegas

so we meet again

you smell just as I remembered

oh and that first glimpse I saw of you

as I flew in

of course you'd show me mandalay bay

fuck you mandalay bay

i never thought i'd be back here

seeing the top golf

and knowing i ran past it

seeing the tropicana

and knowing i ran through it

feeling like i was about to die

vegas i remember your acoustics

with the sound of showering bullets

echoing through the entire city

i remember the mgm grand

and trying to find a place to find shelter

running through restaurant kitchens

nowhere was safe

...

...

vegas, because of you

it's hard to feel safe

i know i know

it's not your fault

but vegas, i trusted you

i trusted you to keep me safe

and i almost fucking died in your arms

these people around me on the streets

don't know the pain you've caused

they don't know how much hurt

and damage you've done

but here we all keep on living

mandalay bay, thanks for caring

for about 5 minutes

with your Vegas Strong banner

but fuck you for trying to move on and take it down

when people are still grieving and suffering

...

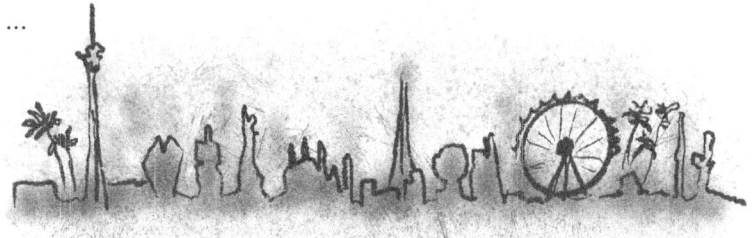

...

i never thought i'd be back here

drinking

going to a concert

living

don't you dare think

even for a minute

that i've forgotten

because even when my mind tries to forget

my body tenses up with the red and blue lights

my body tenses up with the helicopters above

and my body takes on the pain my mind is so

desperately trying to forget

but here i fucking am

living

despite all of this pain

and here i fucking am

standing up and going forward

i'll never forget, vegas

and I'm willing to move forward

just don't you ever fucking let me down, again

dear vegas

one day you'll look back

you'll cry at your pain

but you'll realize the strength that resides within you

for making it to that point

you don't have to be okay today

but you have to make it through to tomorrow

because tomorrow just might be that one day

i want you to see that strength within yourself

like you would point out to a crying best friend

it's hard

to the victims of the

(insert name of recent mass shooting),

embrace the shock and numbness

that you are feeling right now

your brain is trying to protect you

from everything you've just

seen

smelled

felt

heard

seek help for your bleeding psyche

you've been wounded

distract yourself away from the media

and anyone else with a conspiracy theory

or the thought that they know

what you've just experienced

let yourself take

whatever you need from this world

to get you through the day

...

...

the pain will heal into scars one day

but that day isn't today

it might feel like nothing will ever be normal again

and that's kind of true

you've seen too much

you've heard too much

it'll be difficult to find your new sense of normalcy

healing is not linear

and some days you'll feel like a victim

while others you'll feel like a survivor

your pain is valid

heal at your own pace

with love,

a las vegas shooting victim

shared experience

patience

finding it within myself

allowing it to take up space in my life

resting in delayed gratification

pausing

pausing

pausing

digging my heals in the ground

forceful breaks

forceful breaks

breathe in and breathe out

although plans are comfortable

time is merely a construct

sit in the present

with

patience

patience

patience does not

tap

its

foot

in anticipation

halt the shaking leg

halt the shaking hands

sit in it

sit in it

sit with it

patience

healing will occur in its own time

no

matter

the

anticipation

shaky hands

i can see you are in pain

that must be so hard

empathy

empathy

empathy

my words won't erase your trauma

they won't bring back your old life

your loved one

your forgotten happiness

but know

i'll sit with you in

s

i

l

e

n

c

e

and let you process

and think

...

...

and cry

and mourn

without judgement

or motive

and i'll always let you

take the lead

for

your

healing

the therapist

healing

healing is ongoing

when does the healing stop?

i want to be healed

i scream

i want to be fixed

i am done with this pain

i want to be healed

    a gentle hand on my shoulder

    and a Godly voice

        my child

        you will always be healing

        you evolve and grow

        you will hurt

        you will learn lessons

        and you will be healing

        discover the beauty in it

        you will only be healing not healed

        here on this earth

healing not healed

those boots have been through it

dirty without mud

they carried me to safety

they've carried me through the memories

but it's time

time to retire those boots

retire those boots

they are just as broken in as this heart

it's not fair

their life was short

they still had more steps in them

but they remind me of the hurt

the fear

the blood stained night

it's time

finally time

to retire those boots

retired boots

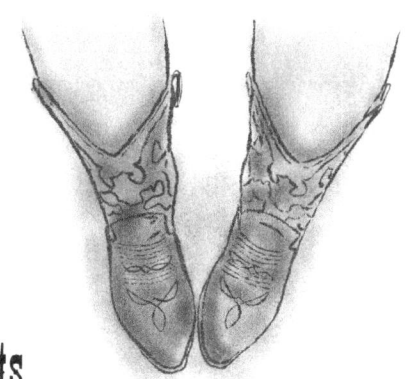

Photography by @ReannaMarchmanPhotography

Dr. Belknap was 21 years old at the time of Route 91 in 2017. She finished her Bachelor's of Psychology degree at University of La Verne in 2018. She then pursued a Master's degree in Counseling Psychology at California Baptist University in 2020, and then completed the qualifications to become a Licensed Marriage and Family Therapist in 2022. She met and married her husband in 2022, and became an instant mother with two bonus children. She continued her educational pursuits with a Doctor of Social Work at California Baptist University. Dr. Belknap successfully defended a dissertation dedicated to the first responders that were at Route 91.

Professionally, Dr. Belknap now runs Healing Not Healed a community based business to encourage healing, promote self-care, inspire resilience, and empower others through speaking engagements, workshops, and merchandise. Personally, Dr. Belknap loves to spend time with her family, creating new things, off-roading, and going to country concerts.

Tikva is a painter, illustrator, and graphic designer who creates art to inspire hope. He uses motifs of rural life as well as ocean themes to express the power of humanity to overcome challenges and live a life of peace.

COUNTRY STRONG

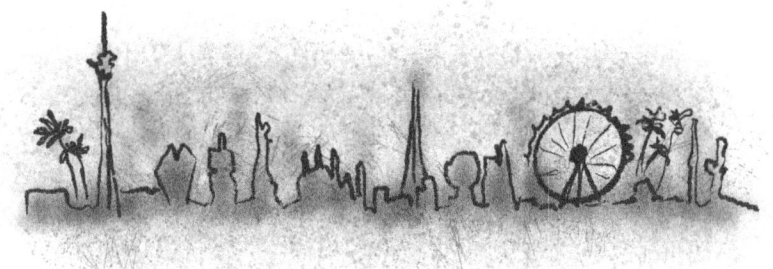

VEGAS STRONG

retired boots
Cover art by Tikva

All rights reserved. No part of this book may be used or reproduced in any manner whatsoever without written permission except in the case of review reprints.

ISBN: 979-8-9906117-1-9
Healing Not Healed

Author: Dr. Morgan Jean Craig Belknap
Artist: Tikva

Dr. Morgan Jean Craig Belknap
The Doctor in Cowgirl Boots
Owner of Healing Not Healed
www.HealingNotHealed.com

Made in the USA
Las Vegas, NV
12 September 2024